True Survival

NANDO PARRADO

CRASH IN THE ANDES

Virginia Lo

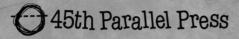
45th Parallel Press

Published in the United States of America by Cherry Lake Publishing
Ann Arbor, Michigan
www.cherrylakepublishing.com

Reading Adviser: Marla Conn MS, Ed., Literacy specialist, Read-Ability, Inc.
Book Designer: Felicia Macheske

Photo Credits: © Gwoeli/Shutterstock.com, cover; © Kay Wiegand/Shutterstock.com, 5; © Fotos593/
Shutterstock.com, 7; © vectorfusionart/Shutterstock.com, 8; © Richie Ji/Shutterstock.com, 11; © Carlos E. Santa
Maria/Shutterstock.com, 12; © Borjaika/Shutterstock.com, 15; © vikiri/Shutterstock.com, 17; © Jenn Mackenzie/
Shutterstock.com, 18; © Simon Kadula/Shutterstock.com, 21; © Cagri Kilicci/Shutterstock.com, 22; © VAKSMAN
VOLODYMYR/Shutterstock.com, 24; © Roman Babakin/Shutterstock.com, 27; © wavebreakmedia/
Shutterstock.com, 29

Graphic Elements Throughout: © Gordan/Shutterstock.com; © adike/Shutterstock.com; © Yure/Shutterstock.com

45th Parallel Press is an imprint of Cherry Lake Publishing.

Library of Congress Cataloging-in-Publication Data

Names: Loh-Hagan, Virginia, author.
Title: Nando Parrado : crash in the Andes / by Virginia Loh-Hagan.
Other titles: Crash in the Andes
Description: Ann Arbor : Cherry Lake Publishing, [2018] | Series: True
 survival | Includes bibliographical references and index.
Identifiers: LCCN 2017031595| ISBN 9781534107762 (hardcover) | ISBN
 9781534109742 (pdf) | ISBN 9781534108752 (pbk.) | ISBN 9781534120730
 (hosted ebook)
Subjects: LCSH: Airplane crash survival—Juvenile literature. | Aircraft
 accidents—Andes Region—Juvenile literature. | Cannibalism—Andes
 Region—Juvenile literature. | Parrado, Nando, 1949-—Juvenile literature.
 | Aircraft accident victims—Uruguay—Biography—Juvenile literature.
Classification: LCC TL553.9 .L643 2018 | DDC 363.12/4092 [B] —dc23
LC record available at https://lccn.loc.gov/2017031595

Cherry Lake Publishing would like to acknowledge the work of The Partnership for 21st Century Skills.
Please visit *www.p21.org* for more information.

Printed in the United States of America
Corporate Graphics

table of contents

chapter one

For Love of the Game

Who is Nando Parrado? What is Uruguayan Air Force Flight 571? Why did Parrado go to Chile?

Nando Parrado was born on December 9, 1949. He was born in Montevideo, Uruguay. Uruguay is in South America. His older sister is Graciela. His younger sister is Susana. His parents are Seler and Eugenia. His family owned **hardware** stores. Hardware includes tools used to build and fix houses.

Parrado went to Stella Maris School. He played sports. He was a good athlete. He was really good at **rugby**. Rugby is a team sport. It's like football and soccer. Parrado played for the school's rugby team. The team was called the Old Christians Club.

Montevideo is the capital of and largest city in Uruguay.

spotlight biography

Sailor Gutzler is a survivor. She was flying from Florida to Illinois. Her father was the pilot. Their plane crashed in Kentucky. Her parents, sister, and cousin died. She broke her wrist. She was 7 years old. She freed herself from the plane. She hiked for a mile. She hiked through thick woods. She hiked in cold weather. She wore shorts and a short-sleeved shirt. She wore one sock. She didn't have any shoes. She hiked in the dark. She walked toward a light. The light was in a house that belonged to Larry Wilkins. Wilkins helped her. He called the police. Gutzler was taken to the hospital. This happened in January 2015. Gutzler was adopted by her half sister.

At first, Parrado studied farming. He did this because of his friends. His friends were farmers. Then, his father talked to him. Parrado changed his mind. He studied business instead.

He studied. He played rugby. He went on dates. He raced cars. He went to parties. He played in the sun. He hung out. He said, "I lived for the moment, **drifting** with the tide, waiting for my future to reveal itself, always happy to let others lead the way." Drifting means going with the flow. Parrado enjoyed life. He didn't have many worries.

Parrado lived close to the beach.

There was a special rugby game. The game was in Chile. The team had to fly there. Parrado got on Uruguayan Air Force Flight 571. The plane was only 4 years old. It only had 792 hours in the air.

The flight had 45 people. Five people were **crew** members. Crew are workers. The other people were the rugby team and their friends and family. Parrado's mother and younger sister were on the flight.

On October 12, 1972, the flight took off. It left Uruguay. It was headed to Santiago, Chile. The trip was supposed to be more than 930 miles (1,497 kilometers). It was supposed to be 4 hours long.

◄ Parrado and his team were excited about the game.

chapter two

A Plane Without Wings

How did the plane crash?

The weather was bad. So the pilot stopped at an airport. He waited for better weather. He took off again.

There were thick clouds. The pilot couldn't see well. He got off track. The plane went over the Andes Mountains. It flew into strong winds. It dropped and shook.

It clipped a peak. This happened at 13,800 feet (4,206 meters). There was a lot of force. The right wing broke off. This left a hole in the plane. The right wing was thrown backward. It hit the tail. The tail broke off. Some people were pulled through the hole. They died.

The Andes are the world's longest mountain range.

The plane clipped another peak. The left wing broke off. The plane's body soared through the air. It crashed at 18,000 feet (5,486 m). It crashed in the Andes. The plane crashed into the **Glacier** of Tears. This is between Chile and Argentina. Glaciers are slow-moving bodies of ice.

The plane hit the ground. It slid down a steep mountain. It moved quickly. It slid into a valley. It slowed down. It slammed into a snowbank. People were thrown forward. They crashed into each other. Many people broke their legs.

This happened on Friday, October 13, 1972.

Many people think Friday the 13th is unlucky.

explained by
science

Avalanches are large amounts of snow falling down a mountainside. They happen in freezing weather. As temperatures rise, snow will sluff. Sluff is loose snow that looks like powder. It begins to slide. Avalanches have three main parts. The starting zone is the most dangerous. It's at the top. This is where snow breaks and slides. The avalanche track is the path. Snow follows this path as it goes downhill. It takes out everything in its way. The runout zone is where the snow and other things finally come to a stop. Avalanches are dangerous. They can be deadly.

chapter three

Desperate Times

What happened to Parrado after the crash? What did the survivors have to do to stay alive?

Parrado said, "Most of us lived by the sea at home. We were never in mountains before or touched snow. One minute we're laughing and joking, and then we're covered in blood and are freezing on this mountain at 11,000 feet with no clear way out."

Parrado's mother and sister died. Parrado passed out. He was in a **coma** for 3 days. Coma means a deep sleep. His friends put ice on his head. The cold treated his head. Parrado woke up. He had a headache. He touched his head. There was blood. His skull had cracked.

Survivors didn't have the right equipment or clothes.

would you?

- **Would you fly on a plane?** Many experts think flying is one of the safest ways to travel. The chance of a person dying on a flight is 1 in 4.7 million. A person's chance of dying in a traffic accident is 1 in 14,000. A person's chance of dying in a lightning strike is 1 in 1.9 million. An expert said, "The most dangerous part of your airline flight is the trip to the airport."

- **Would you fly in a plane without a pilot?** Pilot mistakes are a common cause of crashes. People are working on planes that don't need pilots. These planes are flown by computers. One person on the ground can control several planes.

Twelve people died in the crash. Five people died the next morning. Another person died on the eighth day. Survivors removed the bodies from the plane. The bodies were kept on ice.

Survivors tried to signal for help. Three countries sent search parties. The first search party quit after 8 days. The plane was white. No one could see it in the snow. Parrado said, "No one will find us. We will die here. We must make a plan. We must save ourselves."

Survivors didn't have much food. Parrado spent 3 days eating one chocolate-covered peanut.

Survivors drank melted snow.

Survivors ran out of food. There weren't any plants or animals. They were **desperate**. Desperate means not having other options. They became **cannibals**. Cannibals are people who eat other people. Survivors wanted to stay alive.

They ate the people who had died in the crash. Parrado said, "It had no taste. I chewed, once or twice, then forced myself to swallow. I felt no guilt or shame. I was doing what I had to do to survive."

◄ Cannibalism is taboo. Taboo means it is not accepted by society.

chapter four

Help at Last!

What happened when the avalanche hit? How did Parrado get help?

On October 29, there were **avalanches**. Avalanches are big snow masses that flow quickly down a mountain. Survivors were sleeping in the plane. Avalanches buried them in snow. Eight people died.

Parrado was buried. He waited for help. A friend dug him out. The remaining survivors were stuck in the plane. They were stuck for 3 days. Parrado poked a hole in the roof. He used a cane. This gave them some air. Parrado decided he would go to get help.

Parrado said, "If we were going to die anyway,
I wanted to die trying to get out."

Men on horses helped Parrado and Canessa.

Three men went to get help. They were Parrado, Roberto Canessa, and Antonio Vizintin.

On December 12, 1972, they headed for Chile. Parrado took the lead. He sent Vizintin back early. Parrado and Canessa kept hiking. They hiked 70 miles (113 km). They climbed mountains. They walked in deep snow and ice. They did this for 10 days. They faced many dangers. They almost froze to death. They made a sleeping bag out of plane parts. They couldn't breathe. The air was thin. They found a river. They saw men on horses.

survival tips

SURVIVE AN AIRPLANE CRASH!

- Before your flight takes off, look for the nearest exits. Count the number of rows from your seat to the exits. You may have to move in darkness or thick smoke.

- Sit in the back of the airplane. Some think these are the safest seats.

- Don't be stunned. Listen to the flight crew. Follow instructions.

- Leave your stuff. Focus on getting off the plane. Move fast. The best time to escape is 2 minutes after the crash.

- Signal for help. Search-and-rescue teams will be looking for you.

- Stay with the airplane. Planes are easier to spot than people.

They tried to yell to the men. But the river was too loud. Sergio Catalan was one of the men. He shouted, "Tomorrow!" The next day, Catalan went back for Parrado and Canessa. He threw bread to them. He threw pen and paper tied to a rock.

Parrado wrote, "I come from a plane that fell in the mountains. I am Uruguayan. We have been walking for 10 days. I have a wounded friend up there. In the plane there are still 14 injured people. We have to get out from here quickly and we don't know how. We don't have any food. We are weak. When are you going to come to fetch us? Please, we cannot even walk. Where are we? **SOS**." SOS means help.

◄ Catalan got people to rescue Parrado and Canessa.

chapter five

A Christmas Miracle!

How were the survivors rescued?
What did Parrado do after the crash?

The next morning, Parrado led a team to rescue the others. He guided two helicopters to the crash site. There was bad weather. But they got there. It took 2 trips to get all the survivors.

Survivors were taken to hospitals in Chile. They had many sicknesses. They needed time to heal.

The last 16 survivors were rescued on December 23, 1972. This was more than 2 months after the crash. Their survival became known as a "Christmas miracle."

The rescuers and a priest returned to the site. They buried the bodies. They built a stone pile with an iron cross. They burned the rest of the plane.

The helicopters couldn't touch the ground. They were scared of causing avalanches.

Rest in Peace

There were 27 people on the plane after the crash. Sixteen people survived to be rescued. They were trapped for 72 days. Eleven people died. Numa Turcatti was the last to die before the rescue. He died on the 60th day. He was 25 years old. He graduated from the Jesuit School of the Sacred Heart. He was studying law. The Old Christians rugby team were his friends. They invited him to come. Turcatti didn't play rugby. He played soccer. He was thought to be the toughest and fittest of the group. He didn't get hurt in the plane crash. But he got sick on the mountain. He got weaker. He let himself die.

Parrado gave up his studies. He was sad about losing his mother and sister. He worked in his father's business. He raced cars. He started other businesses. He became a television star. He wrote books about his survival. There was a movie about it. It was called *Alive*. Parrado helped. He gave advice.

He got married. He has 2 daughters. He's returned to the crash site several times. He remembers all the people who died there.

He said, "God has given me the chance to live again. I shouldn't waste this life."

Parrado believes that being a family helped them survive.

Did You Know?

- Captain Julio Cesar Ferradas was the pilot. He flew Uruguayan Air Force Flight 571. He had a lot of experience. He had been an air force pilot for 20 years. He had 5,117 flying hours. He had flown 29 flights across the Andes Mountains. He was 39 years old.

- Nando Parrado's whole name is Fernando Seler Parrado Dolgay.

- The crash is known as the "Andes flight disaster." In South America, it's called the "Miracle of the Andes."

- Adolfo "Fito" Strauch was a survivor. He created special sunglasses. He used sun visors from the pilot's cabin. These sunglasses protected the survivors' eyes.

- Dr. Francisco Nicola was the team doctor. He died in the crash. This left a couple of medical students in charge of healing. They used plane parts to make medical tools.

- Parrado went home 3 months after the crash. His room had been given to his older sister. His clothes were given away. His posters had been removed. His motorbike was sold. His family thought he had died.

- Parrado said, "People always want me to talk about the hunger. But the thirst and the cold were much worse for me. Our lips were cracked and bleeding. And every drop of cold water was painful to drink."

- Survivors collected lipstick from the luggage. They wrote "SOS" on the plane's roof. But the sign couldn't be seen.

Consider This!

Take a Position: Imagine that you were in Parrado's situation. Would you eat the dead bodies to survive? Argue your point with reasons and evidence.

Say What? Read the 45th Parallel Press book about Juliane Koepcke. Explain how Koepcke and Parrado are alike. Explain how they are different.

Think About It! Would you rather be stranded on a mountain during winter or in a jungle during the summer? Explain your thinking. Describe your survival skills.

Learn More

- Parrado, Nando, and Vince Rause. *Miracle in the Andes*. New York: Crown Publishers, 2006.

- Werther, Scott P. *Alive! Airplane Crash in the Andes Mountains*. New York: Children's Press, 2003.

Glossary

avalanches (AV-uh-lanch-iz) big snow masses that flow quickly down a mountain

cannibals (KAN-uh-buhlz) people who eat people

coma (KOH-muh) deep sleep

crew (KROO) people who work on a flight

desperate (DES-pur-it) having no options

drifting (DRIFT-ing) floating or going with the flow

glacier (GLAY-shur) slow-moving body of ice

hardware (HAHRD-wair) tools used to build and fix houses

rugby (RUHG-bee) team sport that is like football and soccer

SOS (ES-oh-es) distress signal, help

Index

About the Author

Dr. Virginia Loh-Hagan is an author, university professor, former classroom teacher, and curriculum designer. The closest she's been to the Andes Mountains is Belize! She lives in San Diego with her very tall husband and very naughty dogs. To learn more about her, visit www.virginialoh.com.